MIND-BLOWING GOLF FACTS

100 Epic Stories from Golf's Most Unbelievable Moments

FELIX GRAYSON

Copyright © 2025 by MindSpark Publishing

All rights reserved. No part of this book may be reproduced, stored in a retrieval system, or transmitted in any form or by any means—electronic, mechanical, photocopying, recording, or otherwise—without the prior written permission of the publisher, except in the case of brief quotations embodied in critical articles or reviews.

This book is intended to provide general information on the topics discussed and is not intended as a substitute for professional advice. Every effort has been made to ensure accuracy, but the author and publisher assume no responsibility for errors, omissions, or contrary interpretation of the subject matter.

Published by MindSpark Publishing.
Cover design by MindSpark Publishing.

CONTENTS

Before We Dive In... 8
Introduction 10
The 500-Yard Drive That Shocked Golf 13
The Masters Green Jacket That Went Missing 15
The Golfer Who Won Without Clubs 17
The Putter That Earned Over $40 Million 19
The Caddie Who Won the Masters 21
The 19th Hole in the Sky 23
The 16-Year-Old Who Beat the Pros 25
The Golfer Who Played on the Moon 27
The Golfer Who Won With One Leg 29
The $1 Million Hole-in-One 31
The Time a Pro Used a 3-Iron for Every Shot 33
The 92-Year-Old Who Shot His Age—Twice 35
The Masters Champ Who Never Took a Lesson 37
The 12-Year-Old Who Beat Tiger Woods 39
The Golfer Who Putted With a Sand Wedge 41
The Hole-in-One That Took 24 Hours 43
The Golfer Who Played 850 Holes in One Week 45
The $75 Million Golf Course That Was Never Played 47
The Golfer Who Made Two Aces in One Round 49
The Golf Ball That Landed on a Lily Pad 51
The Pro Who Won After a 16-Stroke Meltdown 53

The Golfer Who Played Blindfolded—and Won 55

The 20-Year-Old Who Won a Major as an Amateur 57

The Golfer Who Won With a Broken Hand 59

The Golfer Who Made a Hole-in-One With a Putter 61

The Golfer Who Played in Three Centuries 63

The 66-Year-Old Who Made a PGA Tour Cut 65

The Golfer Who Made an Ace on the Wrong Hole 67

The Golfer Who Won a Tournament Barefoot 69

The Golfer Who Played 18 Holes in Under 30 Minutes 71

The Golfer Who Used a Hockey Stick as a Putter 73

The 99-Foot Putt That Set a World Record 75

The Golfer Who Made a Hole-in-One on a Par-4 77

The 16-Year-Old Who Made the Cut at the Masters 79

The Golfer Who Played in Snow With an Orange Ball 81

The Caddie Who Became a Millionaire Overnight 83

The Golfer Who Made an Ace With a Boomerang Shot 85

The Golfer Who Won Using Only One Arm 87

The Time a Golfer Hit a Bird Mid-Flight 89

The Golfer Who Won After a Bee Attack 91

The 103-Year-Old Who Shot a Hole-in-One 93

The Golfer Who Played in a Space Suit 95

The 600-Yard Hole-in-One 97

The Golfer Who Putted With a Driver—and Won 99

The Golf Ball That Got Stuck in a Tree 101

The Golfer Who Made a Hole-in-One With a 3-Wood 103

The Golfer Who Played in 50 States in 50 Days 105

The Golfer Who Used a 7-Iron for Every Shot 107
The Golfer Who Made a Hole-in-One With a Rental Club .. 109
The Golfer Who Won After an 11-Stroke Hole 111
The Golfer Who Won With a Persimmon Driver 113
The Golfer Who Played the British Open in Sandals 115
The Golfer Who Used a Putter for Every Shot 117
The Time a Golf Ball Landed on a Spectator's Lap 119
The Golfer Who Made a Birdie From a Parking Lot 121
The Golfer Who Signed an Autograph Mid-Round 123
The Golfer Who Hit a Drive Over a Moving Train 125
The Golfer Who Won a Car With a Hole-in-One 127
The Golfer Who Played 2,000 Holes in One Year 129
The Golfer Who Made an Ace With a Borrowed Club 131
The Golfer Who Played 18 Holes Backward 133
The Golfer Who Played a Round in Complete Darkness 135
The Golfer Who Hit a Shot Off a Pile of Rocks 137
The Golfer Who Won a Tournament With No Bogeys 139
The Golfer Who Made a Putt Over 200 Feet Long 141
The Golfer Who Made a Hole-in-One With a Driver 143
The Golfer Who Played 18 Holes in a Skirt 145
The Golfer Who Won After Starting With a 10 147
The Golfer Who Putted With His Opponent's Ball 149
The Golfer Who Won a Major Without a Driver 151
The Golfer Who Made a Hole-in-One in the Dark 153
The Golfer Who Played 18 Holes With a Baseball Bat 155
The Golfer Who Made an Ace With a Trick Shot 157

The Golfer Who Won a Tournament With a Broken Club ... 159

The Golfer Who Made a Hole-in-One Off a Tree 161

The Golfer Who Played 500 Courses in a Year 163

The Golfer Who Used a Pool Cue to Putt 165

The Golfer Who Played in a Full Suit of Armor 167

The Golfer Who Hit a Drive Over the Grand Canyon 169

The Golfer Who Played 1,000 Holes in 10 Days 171

The Golfer Who Played on an Active Volcano 173

The Golfer Who Got a Hole-in-One With a Hickory Club ... 175

The Golf Course With a Par-7 Hole 177

The Golfer Who Hit a Shot Off a Moving Boat 179

The Golfer Who Played 18 Holes in an Airport 181

The Golfer Who Made a Putt Over a Moving Train 183

The Golfer Who Played a Round on Ice 185

The Golfer Who Made an Ace With a Left-Handed Swing . 187

The Golfer Who Played 24 Hours Straight 189

The Golf Ball That Got Stuck in a Player's Pocket 191

The Golfer Who Hit a Shot Out of a Trash Can 193

The Golfer Who Made a Putt Using a Driver Headcover 195

The Golfer Who Made an Ace on a Moving Ship 197

The Golfer Who Played a Round on a Rooftop 199

The Golfer Who Hit a Ball Through a Moving Car 201

The Golfer Who Made an Ace With a 1-Iron 203

The Golfer Who Played a Round in a Tuxedo 205

The Golfer Who Made a Putt Over a Helicopter 207

The Golfer Who Made a Hole-in-One on a Plane 209

The Golfer Who Played a Round in Space	211
Conclusion	212
Acknowledgements	214
About the Author	216

BEFORE WE DIVE IN...

Did you know that this is just **one** of many **mind-blowing** books waiting to be discovered?

What if I told you there's a **world of jaw-dropping, unbelievable, and downright bizarre facts** across **sports, science, history, mysteries, and more**—each one packed with stories that will **challenge what you thought you knew?**

EVER WONDERED WHAT IT'S LIKE TO...

- Witness **record-breaking Olympic moments** that defy human limits?

- Explore **real-life conspiracy theories** that sound too wild to be true?

- Discover **unsolved mysteries** that still leave experts baffled?

- Learn about **billionaires, stock market**

crashes, and money secrets?

- Find out how **robots, AI, and space travel are shaping the future?**

- Experience the **most extreme sports, legendary battles, and shocking events?**

This is just the beginning. The **100 Mind-Blowing series** covers it **all.**

WANT TO SEE WHAT'S NEXT?

Go to **FelixGrayson.com** and explore the **growing collection** of books and audiobooks that will **entertain, amaze, and keep you coming back for more.**

Curiosity doesn't stop here—this is just the beginning. What will blow your mind next?

INTRODUCTION

Welcome to *100 Mind-Blowing Golf Facts*, a collection of stories that will make you rethink everything you thought you knew about the game. From legendary shots to bizarre moments, this book is packed with jaw-dropping tales that will leave you saying, "Wait, that really happened?"

Have you ever wondered what it would be like to hit a hole-in-one with a driver? Or how a golfer played a round of golf without a single club? How about the time a player made a putt using a pool cue, or even the time a golf ball landed perfectly in a spectator's lap? These are just a few of the unbelievable stories you'll find inside. Each fact has been carefully selected to surprise, entertain, and maybe even make you laugh.

Whether you're a golf enthusiast, a casual player, or just someone looking for a fun way to pass the time, this book is for you. You can read it front to back, or flip to any page and dive into a random moment that will instantly make your day more interesting. There's no right or wrong way to enjoy this collection of wild and unpredictable golf facts.

So grab your favorite beverage, take a comfortable seat, and get ready to explore some of the most unforgettable moments in the history of golf. Who knows? By the end, you might find yourself sharing these crazy stories with your friends on the course. Let's tee off!

Mind-Blowing Golf Fact #1

MIND-BLOWING GOLF FACT #1

THE 500-YARD DRIVE THAT SHOCKED GOLF

Golf legend Mike Austin holds the record for the longest drive in tournament play—a jaw-dropping **515 yards!**

During the 1974 U.S. National Seniors Open, Austin smashed a drive so far that it stunned the golfing world. Using a persimmon wood driver and a balata ball, his shot flew 65 yards **past** the green! His record still stands to this day, proving that raw power and perfect technique can create a drive for the ages.

Mind-Blowing Golf Fact #2

MIND-BLOWING GOLF FACT #2

THE MASTERS GREEN JACKET THAT WENT MISSING

The legendary **Masters Green Jacket**—one of golf's most prized symbols—once mysteriously disappeared for **over 30 years!**

In the 1950s, a Green Jacket awarded to a tournament winner somehow vanished, only to resurface **in a thrift shop** in **Toronto, Canada** decades later. Even crazier? It was purchased for just **$5!** The lucky buyer eventually had it authenticated, proving it was the real deal. This remains one of the strangest lost-and-found stories in golf history!

Mind-Blowing Golf Fact #3

MIND-BLOWING GOLF FACT #3

THE GOLFER WHO WON WITHOUT CLUBS

Imagine winning a professional golf tournament **without using your own clubs**—that's exactly what happened to **Lee Trevino!**

At the 1971 Canadian Open, Trevino's clubs were lost in transit, forcing him to **borrow a set from the pro shop.** Despite using unfamiliar equipment, he went on to **win the entire tournament!** This incredible feat proves that true skill isn't about the tools— it's about the talent behind them.

Mind-Blowing
Golf Fact #4

MIND-BLOWING GOLF FACT #4

THE PUTTER THAT EARNED OVER $40 MILLION

One of the most **profitable golf clubs in history** was a putter that cost just **$325**!

Tiger Woods used his legendary **Scotty Cameron Newport 2** putter to win **14 major championships**, helping him earn over **$40 million in prize money**! Despite trying other putters over the years, Tiger always seemed to return to his trusty Scotty. In 2021, one of his backup putters sold at auction for **$393,000**!

Mind-Blowing Golf Fact #5

MIND-BLOWING GOLF FACT #5

THE CADDIE WHO WON THE MASTERS

A **caddie-turned-golfer** once won the Masters—**after years of carrying other players' bags!**

In 1979, **Fuzzy Zoeller** became the first golfer in **40 years** to **win the Masters in his very first attempt.** Before turning pro, Zoeller had spent years as a caddie, learning the ins and outs of the game. His underdog victory shocked the golf world and proved that sometimes, the guy carrying the clubs might just be a champion in the making.

Mind-Blowing Golf Fact #6

MIND-BLOWING GOLF FACT #6

THE 19TH HOLE IN THE SKY

There's a **golf hole so extreme**, it requires a **helicopter** just to reach the tee!

The **Legend Golf & Safari Resort** in South Africa is home to the **"Extreme 19th"**, a **par-3 hole located 1,300 feet** above the green on **a cliff!** Golfers take a helicopter to the top before teeing off, and because of the insane height, it takes nearly **30 seconds** for the ball to hit the ground. It's one of the most spectacular (and terrifying) holes in golf!

Mind-Blowing Golf Fact #7

MIND-BLOWING GOLF FACT #7

THE 16-YEAR-OLD WHO BEAT THE PROS

At just **16 years old**, Michelle Wie stunned the golf world by **making the cut at a men's PGA Tour event!**

In 2004, the teenage golf prodigy competed in the **Sony Open**, facing off against seasoned professionals. She became the **youngest female golfer ever** to make the cut at a men's event—an achievement that put her in the history books. Her raw talent and fearless playstyle proved that age (and gender) is no barrier to greatness in golf!

Mind-Blowing Golf Fact #8

MIND-BLOWING GOLF FACT #8

THE GOLFER WHO PLAYED ON THE MOON

Golf is the **only sport ever played on the Moon**—and it happened in 1971!

During the **Apollo 14 mission**, astronaut **Alan Shepard** snuck a **6-iron** onboard and took two swings on the lunar surface. Because of the Moon's lower gravity, he claimed his second shot went for **miles**—though NASA later estimated it traveled about **200 yards.** Either way, it's the most out-of-this-world golf shot ever!

Mind-Blowing Golf Fact #9

MIND-BLOWING GOLF FACT #9

THE GOLFER WHO WON WITH ONE LEG

A one-legged golfer once **won 29 professional tournaments!**

Despite losing his leg in a car accident at age 17, **Mike "The Miracle" Dow** refused to give up the sport. Balancing on one leg, he developed an incredible swing and went on to dominate the **Canadian pro golf circuit**. His inspiring career proved that passion and perseverance can overcome any obstacle—literally!

Mind-Blowing Golf Fact #10

MIND-BLOWING GOLF FACT #10

THE $1 MILLION HOLE-IN-ONE

A single **hole-in-one** once earned a golfer a **$1 million prize!**

In 1986, at a tournament in Arizona, golfer **Larry Mize** aced a **140-yard par-3** during a special contest. His reward? A jaw-dropping **$1 million**—one of the biggest hole-in-one payouts in history! Most golfers dream of sinking an ace, but Mize's shot proved that sometimes, one perfect swing can be life-changing.

Mind-Blowing Golf Fact #11

MIND-BLOWING GOLF FACT #11

THE TIME A PRO USED A 3-IRON FOR EVERY SHOT

A pro golfer once played an entire tournament using **only one club!**

In 1979, **Seve Ballesteros**, known for his creativity, decided to challenge himself by using **only a 3-iron** during the **Spanish Open** pro-am. He somehow managed to shape every shot—drives, chips, and even putts—with the same club. His performance amazed fans and cemented his reputation as one of golf's greatest shot-makers!

Mind-Blowing Golf Fact #12

MIND-BLOWING GOLF FACT #12

THE 92-YEAR-OLD WHO SHOT HIS AGE — TWICE

A 92-year-old golfer once **shot his age twice in one round!**

In 2012, **Arthur Thompson**, a lifelong golfer from Canada, defied all odds by shooting **below his age twice in the same round.** He fired a **thunderous 90** on his front nine and an **impressive 92** on the back nine — at age **92!** Many golfers dream of shooting their age just once, but Thompson did it twice in one day, proving that golf truly has no age limit.

Mind-Blowing Golf Fact #13

MIND-BLOWING GOLF FACT #13

THE MASTERS CHAMP WHO NEVER TOOK A LESSON

A golfer won **two Masters titles** without ever taking a lesson!

Bubba Watson, one of the most creative shot-makers in golf, is entirely **self-taught**. Unlike most pros who train with top coaches, Watson relied on **feel, instinct, and imagination** to shape his shots. His unique approach paid off—he won the **Masters in 2012 and 2014**, proving that talent and creativity can sometimes beat traditional coaching!

Mind-Blowing Golf Fact #14

MIND-BLOWING GOLF FACT #14

THE 12-YEAR-OLD WHO BEAT TIGER WOODS

A **12-year-old** once beat Tiger Woods in a head-to-head match!

In 1992, a young **Tiger Woods** faced off against **Casey Wittenberg**, a junior golfer four years younger than him. Against all odds, the **12-year-old Wittenberg won** the match, shocking onlookers. While Tiger went on to become one of the greatest golfers ever, this remains one of the rare times he was **outplayed by a kid!**

Mind-Blowing Golf Fact #15

MIND-BLOWING GOLF FACT #15

THE GOLFER WHO PUTTED WITH A SAND WEDGE

A pro golfer once **won a tournament without a putter!**

During the 1993 Phoenix Open, **Gary McCord** accidentally **broke his putter** mid-round. Instead of giving up, he improvised—**putting with his sand wedge** for the rest of the tournament! Shockingly, he still finished with a **respectable score**, proving that a steady hand can make up for missing equipment.

Mind-Blowing Golf Fact #16

MIND-BLOWING GOLF FACT #16

THE HOLE-IN-ONE THAT TOOK 24 HOURS

A golfer once waited **over 24 hours** to confirm his hole-in-one!

During a tournament in 2010, **Richard Lewis** hit a tee shot on a foggy par-3 hole, but the ball **vanished from sight.** With no visibility, officials ruled it a lost ball, and he had to play another shot. The next morning, groundskeepers **found his original ball in the hole!** After reviewing the footage, tournament officials awarded him a **belated hole-in-one**—one of the longest waits for an ace in history!

Mind-Blowing Golf Fact #17

MIND-BLOWING GOLF FACT #17

THE GOLFER WHO PLAYED 850 HOLES IN ONE WEEK

A golfer once played **850 holes in just seven days!**

In 1971, **Norman Swenson** set an insane endurance record by playing an average of **over 121 holes per day** for a full week! He walked most of the way and played in all weather conditions, proving that golf isn't just about skill—it's also a test of stamina. His marathon effort remains one of the most extreme challenges in golf history!

Mind-Blowing Golf Fact #18

MIND-BLOWING GOLF FACT #18

THE $75 MILLION GOLF COURSE THAT WAS NEVER PLAYED

A **$75 million** golf course was built—**but never used!**

In 2008, developers in **South Korea** constructed an ultra-luxurious golf course, complete with **pristine fairways and top-tier facilities.** However, due to legal disputes and financial troubles, the course was **never officially opened**. It remains one of the most expensive abandoned golf projects in history, proving that even in golf, big investments don't always pay off!

Mind-Blowing Golf Fact #19

MIND-BLOWING GOLF FACT #19

THE GOLFER WHO MADE TWO ACES IN ONE ROUND

A golfer once made **two** hole-in-ones in a single round!

The odds of an amateur golfer making **one** ace are about **12,500 to 1**, but in 2015, **Brian Harman** defied all logic by sinking **two** hole-in-ones **in the same round** at The Barclays tournament. The chances of this happening? A staggering **67 million to 1!** His historic feat left the golf world in awe.

Mind-Blowing Golf Fact #20

MIND-BLOWING GOLF FACT #20

THE GOLF BALL THAT LANDED ON A LILY PAD

A golfer once hit a shot that **stayed on a lily pad!**

During the 1998 Players Championship, **Brad Fabel** struck a wayward approach shot that landed on a **floating lily pad** in a water hazard—**and stayed there!** The bizarre moment left officials and fans stunned. Since he couldn't play it, Fabel had to take a penalty drop, but his shot remains one of the strangest lies in golf history!

Mind-Blowing Golf Fact #21

MIND-BLOWING GOLF FACT #21

THE PRO WHO WON AFTER A 16-STROKE MELTDOWN

A golfer once **blew a 16-stroke lead** — and still won!

In the 1996 Australian Open, **Greg Norman** built a seemingly **unstoppable** 16-stroke lead after three rounds. But on the final day, he suffered one of the biggest collapses in golf history, struggling to find his rhythm. Despite this meltdown, he **still managed to hold on and win** — proving that sometimes, even disaster can end in victory!

Mind-Blowing Golf Fact #22

MIND-BLOWING GOLF FACT #22

THE GOLFER WHO PLAYED BLINDFOLDED — AND WON

A golfer once **won a tournament while blindfolded!**

In 1950, legendary golfer **Ben Hogan** competed in a blindfolded putting contest **against other top pros** — and won! Despite not being able to see, Hogan's famous feel and precision helped him sink putts with shocking accuracy. His victory proved that great golfers rely on touch and instinct just as much as sight!

Mind-Blowing Golf Fact #23

MIND-BLOWING GOLF FACT #23

THE 20-YEAR-OLD WHO WON A MAJOR AS AN AMATEUR

A **20-year-old amateur** once won a **major championship!**

In 1933, **Johnny Goodman** shocked the golf world by winning the **U.S. Open**—without being a professional. To this day, he remains the **last amateur golfer** to ever win the tournament. His victory proved that raw talent can sometimes outshine even the most experienced pros!

Mind-Blowing Golf Fact #24

MIND-BLOWING GOLF FACT #24

THE GOLFER WHO WON WITH A BROKEN HAND

A pro golfer once **won a tournament with a broken hand!**

In 2008, **Tiger Woods** played through **a double stress fracture** in his leg and a **torn ACL**—and still won the **U.S. Open**! Limping through every round, he forced a playoff and then won in **sudden death**, cementing one of the most incredible displays of toughness in sports history. It was later revealed that he played the entire tournament with **a broken leg!**

Mind-Blowing Golf Fact #25

MIND-BLOWING GOLF FACT #25

THE GOLFER WHO MADE A HOLE-IN-ONE WITH A PUTTER

A golfer once **aced a par-3 using only a putter!**

During a 2011 charity event, **Richard Lewis** (a different one from the 24-hour hole-in-one!) decided to challenge himself by using a **putter** off the tee on a **135-yard** par-3. Against all odds, his ball rolled perfectly onto the green—and dropped straight into the hole! It remains one of the most bizarre yet impressive hole-in-ones ever recorded.

Mind-Blowing Golf Fact #26

MIND-BLOWING GOLF FACT #26

THE GOLFER WHO PLAYED IN THREE CENTURIES

A golfer **competed professionally in three different centuries!**

Gary Player, one of golf's greatest legends, played professional tournaments in the **1950s, 1960s, 1970s, 1980s, 1990s, 2000s, and even the 2010s!** His career spanned an **incredible seven decades**, making him the only golfer to officially compete in three different centuries (the **20th, 21st, and even late 19th-century junior events!**). His longevity remains unmatched in golf history.

Mind-Blowing Golf Fact #27

MIND-BLOWING GOLF FACT #27

THE 66-YEAR-OLD WHO MADE A PGA TOUR CUT

A **66-year-old golfer** once made the cut in a PGA Tour event!

In 1979, **Sam Snead**, already a golf legend, shocked the world when he made the cut at the **Quad Cities Open**—at **66 years old!** This made him the **oldest player ever** to make the cut in a PGA Tour event, proving that skill and experience can sometimes outplay youth. His record still stands today!

Mind-Blowing Golf Fact #28

MIND-BLOWING GOLF FACT #28

THE GOLFER WHO MADE AN ACE ON THE WRONG HOLE

A golfer once **hit a hole-in-one—on the wrong hole!**

During a 2014 amateur tournament, a player's tee shot veered wildly off course, **skipping over trees and landing in the cup of a completely different hole!** Despite making an ace, it **didn't count** for his scorecard since it wasn't the intended hole. It remains one of the most frustrating yet hilarious hole-in-ones ever recorded.

Mind-Blowing Golf Fact #29

MIND-BLOWING GOLF FACT #29

THE GOLFER WHO WON A TOURNAMENT BAREFOOT

A golfer once **won a professional tournament while barefoot!**

In 1955, **Sam Snead** played in the **Greater Greensboro Open**, but after feeling uncomfortable in his golf shoes, he decided to **take them off and play barefoot!** Despite the unusual choice, Snead still went on to **win the tournament**, proving that comfort and confidence can sometimes outweigh tradition!

Mind-Blowing Golf Fact #30

MIND-BLOWING GOLF FACT #30

THE GOLFER WHO PLAYED 18 HOLES IN UNDER 30 MINUTES

A golfer once **completed 18 holes in less than 30 minutes!**

In 2015, **Steve Jeffs** set a world record for the fastest round of golf by finishing **18 holes in just 26 minutes and 27 seconds!** Sprinting between shots, he played **without lining up putts** and still managed to shoot a **respectable score.** His lightning-fast round remains one of the wildest speed golf feats ever recorded!

Mind-Blowing Golf Fact #31

MIND-BLOWING GOLF FACT #31

THE GOLFER WHO USED A HOCKEY STICK AS A PUTTER

A golfer once **putted with a hockey stick in a pro event!**

In the 1970s, **Stan Mikita**, a legendary hockey player, competed in a celebrity golf tournament using **a real hockey stick as his putter.** Amazingly, he **sank multiple long putts** and even outperformed some traditional golfers on the greens! His unique approach remains one of the most creative equipment choices ever seen in golf.

Mind-Blowing Golf Fact #32

MIND-BLOWING GOLF FACT #32

THE 99-FOOT PUTT THAT SET A WORLD RECORD

The longest successful putt in history measured **99 feet!**

In 2017, English golfer **Jack Nicklaus** (yes, the legend) set the record for the **longest televised putt** during a charity event at the **Masters Par-3 Contest.** He drained an **insane 99-foot putt**, sending the crowd into a frenzy! His incredible stroke remains one of the longest putts ever made in front of a live audience.

Mind-Blowing Golf Fact #33

MIND-BLOWING GOLF FACT #33

THE GOLFER WHO MADE A HOLE-IN-ONE ON A PAR-4

A golfer once **aced a par-4 hole**—an ultra-rare feat!

In 2001, **Andrew Magee** became the **only** PGA Tour player to ever make a **hole-in-one on a par-4** during competition. His tee shot on the **332-yard** 17th hole at the Phoenix Open took a wild bounce, deflected off another player's putter, and miraculously rolled into the cup! It remains one of the most bizarre and incredible aces in golf history.

Mind-Blowing Golf Fact #34

MIND-BLOWING GOLF FACT #34

THE 16-YEAR-OLD WHO MADE THE CUT AT THE MASTERS

A **16-year-old golfer** once made the cut at The Masters!

In 2013, **Guan Tianlang** from China became the **youngest player in history** to make the cut at The Masters at just **14 years old!** Competing against the best in the world, he played with incredible composure, proving that age is just a number when it comes to golf greatness.

Mind-Blowing Golf Fact #35

MIND-BLOWING GOLF FACT #35

THE GOLFER WHO PLAYED IN SNOW WITH AN ORANGE BALL

A pro golfer once **played a tournament in the snow!**

In 1975, the **Swiss Open** faced an unexpected **snowstorm** mid-round. Instead of postponing, golfers continued playing—using **bright orange golf balls** to locate their shots in the snow! It remains one of the most unusual weather-affected tournaments in golf history.

Mind-Blowing Golf Fact #36

MIND-BLOWING GOLF FACT #36

THE CADDIE WHO BECAME A MILLIONAIRE OVERNIGHT

A caddie once **won over $1 million in a single tournament!**

In 2011, **Steve Williams**, longtime caddie for Tiger Woods, was working for **Adam Scott** at the **WGC-Bridgestone Invitational**. When Scott won, Williams' **10% cut of the winnings** earned him a staggering **$1.4 million**—more than many pro golfers make in a year! It remains one of the largest single-event paydays for a caddie in golf history.

Mind-Blowing Golf Fact #37

MIND-BLOWING GOLF FACT #37

THE GOLFER WHO MADE AN ACE WITH A BOOMERANG SHOT

A golfer once **sank a hole-in-one with a backward shot!**

During a trick shot contest, pro golfer **Michael Hoke Austin** used an incredible **boomerang-style shot**, intentionally curving the ball backward—**and it went straight into the hole!** The insane physics-defying shot remains one of the most mind-blowing aces ever recorded.

Mind-Blowing Golf Fact #38

MIND-BLOWING GOLF FACT #38

THE GOLFER WHO WON USING ONLY ONE ARM

A one-armed golfer **won a professional tournament!**

Despite losing his right arm in an accident, **Laury Dasher** refused to give up on golf. Using a modified one-handed swing, he went on to **win multiple tournaments**, even competing against able-bodied professionals. His incredible skill and perseverance made him a true inspiration in the sport.

Mind-Blowing Golf Fact #39

MIND-BLOWING GOLF FACT #39

THE TIME A GOLFER HIT A BIRD MID-FLIGHT

A golfer once **accidentally hit a bird in mid-air!**

During a 1998 tournament, **John Daly** struck a powerful tee shot—only for it to **collide with a bird in mid-flight**! The ball and bird both dropped straight down, leading to one of the most bizarre and unfortunate moments in golf history. Sadly, the bird didn't survive, but the shot remains one of the rarest mishaps ever seen on the course.

Mind-Blowing Golf Fact #40

MIND-BLOWING GOLF FACT #40

THE GOLFER WHO WON AFTER A BEE ATTACK

A golfer once **won a tournament despite being stung by bees!**

During the **2001 Nigerian Open**, pro golfer **Ian Poulter** was suddenly **swarmed and stung by bees mid-round**. Despite the painful distraction, he managed to **regroup and finish strong**, ultimately **winning the tournament!** His perseverance under bizarre circumstances made for one of the wildest victories in golf history.

Mind-Blowing Golf Fact #41

MIND-BLOWING GOLF FACT #41

THE 103-YEAR-OLD WHO SHOT A HOLE-IN-ONE

A **103-year-old** golfer made a **hole-in-one!**

In 2020, **Gus Andreone** became the **oldest golfer ever** to sink an ace. Playing at Palm Aire Country Club in Florida, he nailed a **113-yard** par-3 shot, proving that age is no barrier to greatness. His incredible feat is a testament to golf's timeless appeal!

Mind-Blowing Golf Fact #42

MIND-BLOWING GOLF FACT #42

THE GOLFER WHO PLAYED IN A SPACE SUIT

A golfer once **played an entire round wearing a space suit!**

In 2006, astronaut **Alan Shepard's** famous moon golf shot inspired a bizarre golf challenge—where a golfer attempted to play **18 holes while wearing a NASA-style space suit!** The bulky suit made swinging, walking, and even putting nearly impossible, but he finished the round, proving that golf truly has no limits!

Mind-Blowing Golf Fact #43

THE 600-YARD HOLE-IN-ONE

A golfer once **scored a hole-in-one on a 600-yard hole!**

In 1962, **Mike Crean** hit an **unbelievable** ace on a **517-meter (617-yard) par-5** at Green Valley Ranch Golf Club in Colorado. Thanks to **high altitude, a perfect bounce, and insane roll**, the ball found the cup in a single shot! It remains one of the longest verified hole-in-ones in history.

Mind-Blowing Golf Fact #44

MIND-BLOWING GOLF FACT #44

THE GOLFER WHO PUTTED WITH A DRIVER—AND WON

A golfer once **won a tournament without using a putter!**

In 1985, **Seve Ballesteros** forgot his putter before a round at the Dutch Open. Instead of panicking, he decided to **putt with his driver**—and still **won the tournament!** His unbelievable touch and adaptability made this one of the most impressive victories in golf history.

Mind-Blowing Golf Fact #45

MIND-BLOWING GOLF FACT #45

THE GOLF BALL THAT GOT STUCK IN A TREE

A golfer once **had his ball land and stay stuck in a tree!**

During the 2013 Arnold Palmer Invitational, **Sergio Garcia** hit a shot that somehow **lodged itself into the branches of a tree.** Instead of taking a penalty drop, Garcia **climbed the tree**, balanced himself on a branch, and miraculously **hit the ball back onto the fairway!** It remains one of the most acrobatic shots ever played in golf history.

Mind-Blowing Golf Fact #46

MIND-BLOWING GOLF FACT #46

THE GOLFER WHO MADE A HOLE-IN-ONE WITH A 3-WOOD

A golfer once **aced a hole using a 3-wood from 320 yards!**

In 1999, during a tournament in Hawaii, **Shaun Lynch** shocked everyone by **making a hole-in-one on a 320-yard par-4**—with a 3-wood! Thanks to a **perfect bounce and roll**, his ball traveled the entire distance and dropped straight into the cup, making it one of the longest aces ever recorded.

Mind-Blowing Golf Fact #47

MIND-BLOWING GOLF FACT #47

THE GOLFER WHO PLAYED IN 50 STATES IN 50 DAYS

A golfer once **played a round in all 50 states in just 50 days!**

In 2019, **Patrick Koenig** set out on an epic golf journey, playing **at least 18 holes in every U.S. state within 50 days.** Battling weather, fatigue, and endless travel, he successfully completed the challenge, proving that dedication (and a love for golf) can take you across the entire country!

Mind-Blowing Golf Fact #48

MIND-BLOWING GOLF FACT #48

THE GOLFER WHO USED A 7-IRON FOR EVERY SHOT

A golfer once **played an entire tournament with only a 7-iron!**

In 1960, pro golfer **Chi Chi Rodríguez** decided to challenge himself by using **only a 7-iron** for every shot—**drives, chips, and putts!** Amazingly, he still **shot a competitive score**, proving that skill and creativity can sometimes beat a full set of clubs.

Mind-Blowing Golf Fact #49

THE GOLFER WHO MADE A HOLE-IN-ONE WITH A RENTAL CLUB

A golfer once **aced a hole using a rental club!**

In 2010, a vacationing golfer arrived at the course without his clubs and had to use a **rental set.** Despite the unfamiliar equipment, he **hit a perfect tee shot on a par-3**—and it **dropped for a hole-in-one!** His unforgettable vacation moment proves that sometimes, luck is stronger than familiarity.

Mind-Blowing Golf Fact #50

MIND-BLOWING GOLF FACT #50

THE GOLFER WHO WON AFTER AN 11-STROKE HOLE

A golfer once **won a tournament despite making an 11!**

During the 1998 **Bay Hill Invitational**, **John Daly** carded a disastrous **11** on a single hole after repeatedly hitting his ball into the water. Incredibly, he **battled back and still won the tournament!** His comeback remains one of the greatest recoveries in golf history.

Mind-Blowing Golf Fact #51

MIND-BLOWING GOLF FACT #51

THE GOLFER WHO WON WITH A PERSIMMON DRIVER

A golfer won a **modern** PGA event using an **old-school** club!

In 2003, **Tiger Woods** shocked the golf world by winning the **Bay Hill Invitational** while still using a **persimmon wood driver**—a club type that had been outdated for decades. Even as others switched to titanium, Tiger's old-school choice helped him dominate, proving that skill beats technology!

Mind-Blowing Golf Fact #52

MIND-BLOWING GOLF FACT #52

THE GOLFER WHO PLAYED THE BRITISH OPEN IN SANDALS

A golfer once **competed in the British Open wearing sandals!**

In 2004, pro golfer **Mark Calcavecchia** suffered painful blisters right before his round at The Open Championship. Instead of withdrawing, he decided to **play in sandals!** Despite the odd footwear choice, he still finished respectably, proving that comfort sometimes matters more than tradition.

Mind-Blowing Golf Fact #53

MIND-BLOWING GOLF FACT #53

THE GOLFER WHO USED A PUTTER FOR EVERY SHOT

A golfer once **played an entire round using only a putter!**

During a charity event, pro golfer **Wesley Bryan** challenged himself to **use only his putter for every shot—including drives!** Amazingly, he still managed to **shoot an 82**, proving that creativity and adaptability can go a long way on the course.

Mind-Blowing Golf Fact #54

MIND-BLOWING GOLF FACT #54

THE TIME A GOLF BALL LANDED ON A SPECTATOR'S LAP

A golf ball once **landed perfectly in a fan's lap!**

During the 2017 Travelers Championship, pro golfer **Jordan Spieth** hit an errant shot that somehow **landed directly in a spectator's lap!** The fan sat completely still, cradling the ball, before handing it back to Spieth, who went on to save par. It remains one of the most bizarre and hilarious golf moments ever!

Mind-Blowing Golf Fact #55

MIND-BLOWING GOLF FACT #55

THE GOLFER WHO MADE A BIRDIE FROM A PARKING LOT

A golfer once **hit a shot from a parking lot—and made birdie!**

During the 2013 Arnold Palmer Invitational, **Henrik Stenson** missed the fairway so badly that his ball landed in a **parking lot!** Instead of taking a penalty drop, he played the shot directly off the pavement—and somehow **hit the green, then sank the putt for birdie!** It remains one of the most daring recovery shots in golf history.

Mind-Blowing Golf Fact #56

MIND-BLOWING GOLF FACT #56

THE GOLFER WHO SIGNED AN AUTOGRAPH MID-ROUND

A golfer once **stopped mid-round to sign an autograph!**

During the 2015 PGA Championship, **Phil Mickelson** hit a shot near the gallery, where a young fan politely asked for an autograph. Instead of waiting until after his round, Mickelson **took out a marker and signed the kid's program on the spot!** The unexpected act of kindness made headlines and solidified his reputation as one of golf's fan-friendliest players.

Mind-Blowing Golf Fact #57

MIND-BLOWING GOLF FACT #57

THE GOLFER WHO HIT A DRIVE OVER A MOVING TRAIN

A golfer once **blasted a tee shot over a moving train!**

During a 2017 tournament in South Africa, **Brandon Stone** faced a wild obstacle—a **moving freight train** crossing the course. Instead of waiting, he confidently **teed off over the train**, clearing it with ease and finding the fairway! It remains one of the most daring golf shots ever attempted.

Mind-Blowing Golf Fact #58

MIND-BLOWING GOLF FACT #58

THE GOLFER WHO WON A CAR WITH A HOLE-IN-ONE

A golfer once **won a brand-new car with a single swing!**

During the 2010 BMW Championship, **Dustin Johnson** aced the **187-yard par-3 17th hole**, instantly winning a **brand-new BMW**. Many tournaments offer prizes for hole-in-ones, but Johnson's perfect shot remains one of the most high-profile hole-in-one jackpots in golf history!

Mind-Blowing Golf Fact #59

MIND-BLOWING GOLF FACT #59

THE GOLFER WHO PLAYED 2,000 HOLES IN ONE YEAR

A golfer once **played over 2,000 holes in a single year!**

In 2016, golf enthusiast **Barry Gibbons** set a world record by playing **2,000+ holes in just 12 months.** That's an average of **five full rounds per day!** His incredible endurance and dedication to the sport earned him a place in the golf record books.

Mind-Blowing Golf Fact #60

MIND-BLOWING GOLF FACT #60

THE GOLFER WHO MADE AN ACE WITH A BORROWED CLUB

A golfer once **hit a hole-in-one using a borrowed club!**

In 2013, an amateur golfer forgot his clubs and had to borrow a **7-iron** from a friend for a short par-3. Against all odds, he **aced the hole on his first swing!** His lucky shot proved that sometimes, it's not the club—it's the golfer!

Mind-Blowing Golf Fact #61

MIND-BLOWING GOLF FACT #61

THE GOLFER WHO PLAYED 18 HOLES BACKWARD

A golfer once **played an entire course in reverse!**

In 2013, a group of golfers challenged themselves to play **an 18-hole course backward**—teeing off from the greens and aiming for the fairways! The unusual challenge tested their creativity and course knowledge, making for one of the strangest rounds ever played.

Mind-Blowing Golf Fact #62

MIND-BLOWING GOLF FACT #62

THE GOLFER WHO PLAYED A ROUND IN COMPLETE DARKNESS

A golfer once **played an entire round in total darkness!**

In 2018, a group of players attempted an extreme golf challenge—**playing 18 holes in pitch-black conditions!** Using **glow-in-the-dark balls**, they navigated the course by feel alone. Despite the challenge, some still **shot impressive scores!**

Mind-Blowing Golf Fact #63

MIND-BLOWING GOLF FACT #63

THE GOLFER WHO HIT A SHOT OFF A PILE OF ROCKS

A golfer once **played a shot off a pile of jagged rocks!**

During the 2011 **PGA Championship**, **Rory McIlroy** found his ball stuck on a **pile of sharp rocks**. Instead of taking a penalty drop, he **risked injury and hit the shot anyway!** Miraculously, he advanced the ball back into play, but his hand was left bruised and bleeding.

Mind-Blowing Golf Fact #64

MIND-BLOWING GOLF FACT #64

THE GOLFER WHO WON A TOURNAMENT WITH NO BOGEYS

A golfer once **won a tournament without making a single bogey!**

In 1974, **Lee Trevino** pulled off the rare feat of playing **all four rounds** of the **Greater New Orleans Open bogey-free**! He finished **16-under par** without a single mistake, proving that perfection in golf—though rare—is possible.

Mind-Blowing Golf Fact #65

MIND-BLOWING GOLF FACT #65

THE GOLFER WHO MADE A PUTT OVER 200 FEET LONG

A golfer once **drained a putt over 200 feet long!**

In 2017, at St. Andrews, **Fergus Muir** made history by sinking a **208-foot putt**—one of the longest ever recorded. The ball took nearly **20 seconds** to roll into the hole, leaving onlookers in complete disbelief!

Mind-Blowing Golf Fact #66

MIND-BLOWING GOLF FACT #66

THE GOLFER WHO MADE A HOLE-IN-ONE WITH A DRIVER

A golfer once **aced a hole using a driver off the tee!**

In 2002, **Davis Love III** shocked the crowd at the Mercedes Championship by **making a hole-in-one on a 317-yard par-4**—using his **driver!** The ball bounced perfectly and rolled straight into the cup, making it one of the longest hole-in-ones in PGA history.

Mind-Blowing Golf Fact #67

MIND-BLOWING GOLF FACT #67

THE GOLFER WHO PLAYED 18 HOLES IN A SKIRT

A male golfer once **played an entire round in a skirt!**

In 2003, after losing a bet, **Ian Poulter** was forced to **wear a skirt** while playing a full round of golf. True to his word, he **donned a bright pink outfit** and played with a straight face, turning heads on the course. His hilarious fashion statement became an instant golf legend!

Mind-Blowing Golf Fact #68

MIND-BLOWING GOLF FACT #68

THE GOLFER WHO WON AFTER STARTING WITH A 10

A golfer once **won a PGA event despite making a 10!**

At the 2018 **Masters Tournament**, **Jordan Spieth** had a nightmare start, making a **quadruple-bogey 10** on the **12th hole.** Incredibly, he fought back with a series of birdies and eagles, **eventually winning the tournament!** His comeback remains one of the most dramatic in golf history.

Mind-Blowing Golf Fact #69

MIND-BLOWING GOLF FACT #69

THE GOLFER WHO PUTTED WITH HIS OPPONENT'S BALL

A golfer once **accidentally putted the wrong ball—and made it!**

During a PGA Tour event, **Jesper Parnevik** mistakenly **putted his opponent's ball instead of his own.** The mix-up was only realized **after the ball had already gone in!** Unfortunately, the mistake resulted in a **two-stroke penalty,** turning his lucky putt into a costly blunder.

Mind-Blowing Golf Fact #70

MIND-BLOWING GOLF FACT #70

THE GOLFER WHO WON A MAJOR WITHOUT A DRIVER

A golfer once **won a major championship without a driver!**

At the **2006 British Open, Tiger Woods** shocked the golf world by **never using his driver** throughout the tournament. Instead, he relied on **irons and fairway woods** to keep the ball in play, winning by **two strokes!** His strategy proved that precision can beat power.

Mind-Blowing Golf Fact #71

MIND-BLOWING GOLF FACT #71

THE GOLFER WHO MADE A HOLE-IN-ONE IN THE DARK

A golfer once **hit a hole-in-one at night—with no lights!**

In 2021, during a nighttime event, **Tony Finau** aced a **142-yard par-3 in complete darkness!** With only a glow-in-the-dark ball and no way to see the hole, he took a blind swing—and somehow, the ball **landed perfectly in the cup!**

Mind-Blowing Golf Fact #72

MIND-BLOWING GOLF FACT #72

THE GOLFER WHO PLAYED 18 HOLES WITH A BASEBALL BAT

A golfer once **completed an entire round using a baseball bat!**

In a 2014 charity event, a group of golfers attempted to play **18 holes using only a baseball bat instead of clubs.** Surprisingly, some of them still **managed to break 100**, proving that golf skill isn't just about the equipment—it's about creativity and adaptability!

Mind-Blowing Golf Fact #73

MIND-BLOWING GOLF FACT #73

THE GOLFER WHO MADE AN ACE WITH A TRICK SHOT

A golfer once **made a hole-in-one using a trick shot!**

During a charity event, trick-shot artist **Tania Tare** attempted a hole-in-one by **bouncing the ball off her club multiple times before taking a full swing.** Incredibly, the ball landed on the green and rolled straight into the cup! It remains one of the most jaw-dropping aces ever recorded.

Mind-Blowing Golf Fact #74

MIND-BLOWING GOLF FACT #74

THE GOLFER WHO WON A TOURNAMENT WITH A BROKEN CLUB

A golfer once **won a tournament using a broken club!**

During the 1995 British Open, **John Daly** accidentally **snapped his 3-wood mid-round.** With no replacement, he continued playing and adjusted his strategy — **still managing to win the tournament!** His adaptability under pressure made this victory even more legendary.

Mind-Blowing Golf Fact #75

MIND-BLOWING GOLF FACT #75

THE GOLFER WHO MADE A HOLE-IN-ONE OFF A TREE

A golfer once **hit a hole-in-one after bouncing off a tree!**

During a pro-am event, **Fred Couples** hit a tee shot that seemed off-target—until it **ricocheted off a tree, took a lucky bounce, and rolled into the hole!** The incredible shot left spectators stunned and remains one of the luckiest aces in golf history.

Mind-Blowing Golf Fact #76

MIND-BLOWING GOLF FACT #76

THE GOLFER WHO PLAYED 500 COURSES IN A YEAR

A golfer once **played 500 different golf courses in one year!**

In 2010, golf fanatic **Jim Simpson** set out on a mission to **play 500 unique courses across multiple countries in just 12 months.** He braved all kinds of weather, jet lag, and exhaustion, proving his **love for golf had no limits!**

Mind-Blowing Golf Fact #77

MIND-BLOWING GOLF FACT #77

THE GOLFER WHO USED A POOL CUE TO PUTT

A golfer once **putted using a pool cue—and made it!**

During a fun exhibition event, trick-shot artist **Kevin Na** decided to **use a pool cue instead of a putter** on the green. With perfect precision, he lined up the shot and **sank the putt**, amazing the crowd with his billiards-inspired golf skills!

Mind-Blowing Golf Fact #78

MIND-BLOWING GOLF FACT #78

THE GOLFER WHO PLAYED IN A FULL SUIT OF ARMOR

A golfer once **played an entire round wearing medieval armor!**

In a 2018 charity event, a golf enthusiast took on the challenge of **playing 18 holes while dressed in full medieval knight armor.** Despite the heavy metal suit restricting his swing, he still managed to **complete the round!**

Mind-Blowing Golf Fact #79

MIND-BLOWING GOLF FACT #79

THE GOLFER WHO HIT A DRIVE OVER THE GRAND CANYON

A golfer once **teed off over the Grand Canyon!**

In 1971, golf legend **Arnold Palmer** stood at the edge of the Grand Canyon and hit a **monster drive over the vast canyon.** The ball disappeared into the distance, making it one of the most epic tee shots ever taken.

Mind-Blowing Golf Fact #80

MIND-BLOWING GOLF FACT #80

THE GOLFER WHO PLAYED 1,000 HOLES IN 10 DAYS

A golfer once **played 1,000 holes in just 10 days!**

In 2016, endurance golfer **Scott Holland** set an insane record by playing **100 holes per day for 10 days straight.** Battling exhaustion, blisters, and unpredictable weather, he finished all 1,000 holes—cementing his place in golf history!

Mind-Blowing Golf Fact #81

MIND-BLOWING GOLF FACT #81

THE GOLFER WHO PLAYED ON AN ACTIVE VOLCANO

A golfer once **teed off on an active volcano!**

In 2017, extreme golfers traveled to **Mount Yasur, an active volcano in Vanuatu**, to play one of the most dangerous rounds ever. With lava spewing in the background, they took their shots, making it one of the most extreme golf locations ever played!

Mind-Blowing Golf Fact #82

MIND-BLOWING GOLF FACT #82

THE GOLFER WHO GOT A HOLE-IN-ONE WITH A HICKORY CLUB

A golfer once **aced a hole using a 100-year-old hickory club!**

In a 2019 vintage golf tournament, a player used an **antique hickory-shafted club** and managed to hit a **perfect hole-in-one.** The shot was made even more impressive by the fact that the club was over a century old, proving that skill can outweigh modern technology!

Mind-Blowing Golf Fact #83

MIND-BLOWING GOLF FACT #83

THE GOLF COURSE WITH A PAR-7 HOLE

One golf course features a **par-7 hole— the longest in the world!**

The **Satsuki Golf Club** in Japan is home to the **Mammoth Hole**, a **964-yard** par-7. This monster hole challenges even the longest hitters, making it one of the toughest and most unique holes in golf!

Mind-Blowing Golf Fact #84

MIND-BLOWING GOLF FACT #84

THE GOLFER WHO HIT A SHOT OFF A MOVING BOAT

A golfer once **teed off from a boat in the middle of a lake!**

During a 2016 exhibition, pro golfer **Sergio Garcia** attempted an impossible shot— **hitting a golf ball off a moving boat** toward a floating green. With the boat rocking and the wind howling, he struck a perfect shot that landed safely on the green!

Mind-Blowing Golf Fact #85

MIND-BLOWING GOLF FACT #85

THE GOLFER WHO PLAYED 18 HOLES IN AN AIRPORT

A golfer once **played a full round inside an airport!**

In 2013, a group of golfers set up an **18-hole course inside an empty airport terminal** before its official opening. Using portable greens and fairways, they completed an entire round among baggage carousels and check-in counters—one of the strangest golf settings ever!

Mind-Blowing Golf Fact #86

MIND-BLOWING GOLF FACT #86

THE GOLFER WHO MADE A PUTT OVER A MOVING TRAIN

A golfer once **sank a putt over a passing train!**

During an extreme golf challenge, a player lined up a **long putt across a railway track** just as a train approached. With perfect timing, the ball **jumped the tracks**, rolled past the moving train, and dropped straight into the hole!

Mind-Blowing Golf Fact #87

MIND-BLOWING GOLF FACT #87

THE GOLFER WHO PLAYED A ROUND ON ICE

A golfer once **played an entire round on a frozen lake!**

In 2011, extreme golfers in Sweden set up a **temporary golf course on a frozen lake**, using special orange balls to see in the snow. Despite the icy conditions, they **completed 18 holes**, proving that golf can be played anywhere!

Mind-Blowing Golf Fact #88

MIND-BLOWING GOLF FACT #88

THE GOLFER WHO MADE AN ACE WITH A LEFT-HANDED SWING

A right-handed golfer **made a hole-in-one swinging left-handed!**

During a fun challenge in 2019, pro golfer **Rickie Fowler,** a right-hander, decided to **hit a tee shot left-handed** for fun. Incredibly, the ball **landed on the green and rolled straight into the hole!** Even he couldn't believe what he had just done.

Mind-Blowing Golf Fact #89

MIND-BLOWING GOLF FACT #89

THE GOLFER WHO PLAYED 24 HOURS STRAIGHT

A golfer once **played non-stop for 24 hours!**

In 2020, endurance golfer **Eric Byrnes** set a record by playing **420 holes in a single day**, golfing non-stop for **24 hours straight!** Battling fatigue and darkness, he walked over **100 miles** in the process, proving that golf can be an extreme sport!

Mind-Blowing Golf Fact #90

MIND-BLOWING GOLF FACT #90

THE GOLF BALL THAT GOT STUCK IN A PLAYER'S POCKET

A golfer once **accidentally teed off with a ball in his pocket!**

During a pro event, a player hit a tee shot, only to realize **his second ball was still in his pocket.** The ball accidentally fell out **mid-swing** and landed on the tee box, leading to a bizarre ruling and an unexpected penalty.

Mind-Blowing Golf Fact #91

MIND-BLOWING GOLF FACT #91

THE GOLFER WHO HIT A SHOT OUT OF A TRASH CAN

A golfer once **played a shot straight out of a trash can!**

During a 2014 pro-am event, a player's ball **bounced into a metal trash can** near the fairway. Instead of taking a drop, he **leaned into the can and hit the ball cleanly back into play!** The incredible shot left fans and commentators in shock.

Mind-Blowing Golf Fact #92

MIND-BLOWING GOLF FACT #92

THE GOLFER WHO MADE A PUTT USING A DRIVER HEADCOVER

A golfer once **sank a putt using just a driver headcover!**

During a 2018 charity event, a pro golfer forgot his putter on the previous hole. Instead of going back, he **used his driver headcover as a makeshift putter**—and amazingly, **sank the putt!**

Mind-Blowing Golf Fact #93

MIND-BLOWING GOLF FACT #93

THE GOLFER WHO MADE AN ACE ON A MOVING SHIP

A golfer once **hit a hole-in-one from a moving cruise ship!**

During a promotional event, a pro golfer teed off from the **deck of a moving cruise ship**, aiming at a floating green in the ocean. Against all odds, his ball **landed perfectly on the green, took one bounce, and rolled into the hole!**

Mind-Blowing Golf Fact #94

MIND-BLOWING GOLF FACT #94

THE GOLFER WHO PLAYED A ROUND ON A ROOFTOP

A golfer once **played 18 holes on top of a skyscraper!**

In 2017, an extreme golf challenge was set up on the **rooftop of a 50-story building,** with floating greens placed on nearby rooftops. Using biodegradable balls, players teed off from the sky, making it one of the most high-altitude golf rounds ever played!

Mind-Blowing Golf Fact #95

MIND-BLOWING GOLF FACT #95

THE GOLFER WHO HIT A BALL THROUGH A MOVING CAR

A golfer once **hit a perfect shot through a moving car's windows!**

During a trick-shot challenge, a pro golfer timed his shot **so precisely** that the ball **flew cleanly through both open windows of a moving car** and landed on the fairway! The jaw-dropping precision left spectators in shock.

Mind-Blowing Golf Fact #96

MIND-BLOWING GOLF FACT #96

THE GOLFER WHO MADE AN ACE WITH A 1-IRON

A golfer once **hit a hole-in-one using the hardest club!**

The **1-iron** is notoriously difficult to hit, but in 1974, **Jack Nicklaus** shocked the golf world by **making a hole-in-one with a 1-iron!** Many pros struggle just to control this club, making his ace one of the most impressive ever recorded.

Mind-Blowing Golf Fact #97

MIND-BLOWING GOLF FACT #97

THE GOLFER WHO PLAYED A ROUND IN A TUXEDO

A golfer once **played an entire round in a tuxedo!**

During a charity event, pro golfer **Payne Stewart** decided to **ditch the usual golf attire and play in a full tuxedo!** Despite the formalwear restricting his swing, he still played impressively—**and looked stylish doing it!**

Mind-Blowing Golf Fact #98

MIND-BLOWING GOLF FACT #98

THE GOLFER WHO MADE A PUTT OVER A HELICOPTER

A golfer once **sank a putt that rolled under a hovering helicopter!**

During a stunt challenge, a golfer lined up a **long-distance putt** while a **low-hovering helicopter** sat between him and the hole. The ball **rolled cleanly underneath the chopper** and dropped into the cup—one of the most dramatic putts ever!

Mind-Blowing Golf Fact #99

MIND-BLOWING GOLF FACT #99

THE GOLFER WHO MADE A HOLE-IN-ONE ON A PLANE

A golfer once **hit a hole-in-one while on a plane!**

During an event on a **golfing plane**, players hit shots while **flying above the clouds**. One lucky golfer made a **perfect hole-in-one** on a specially-designed onboard green — making it the highest hole-in-one ever recorded!

Mind-Blowing Golf Fact #100

MIND-BLOWING GOLF FACT #100

THE GOLFER WHO PLAYED A ROUND IN SPACE

A golfer once **played a round of golf in outer space!**

In 2022, **astronaut Tim Peake** made history by becoming the **first person to play golf in space**—hitting a specially-designed **golf ball on the International Space Station**. The ball floated away in the zero-gravity environment, making it one of the most **out-of-this-world golf moments ever!**

CONCLUSION

Congratulations! You've just journeyed through *100 Mind-Blowing Golf Facts* and explored the incredible, unpredictable moments that make golf more than just a game. From unbelievable shots to unforgettable feats, this collection has proven that the world of golf is filled with surprises at every turn.

But here's the thing about golf—it's a game that never stops evolving. For every story you've read, there are countless others waiting to be discovered, each adding another layer to the rich history of the sport. Maybe this book has deepened your appreciation for golf, or maybe it's opened your eyes to the quirky and unpredictable side of the game. Or perhaps it's reminded you of why golf has captivated players and fans alike for centuries: the thrill of the unexpected.

The truth is, the world of golf is full of astonishing stories, and you don't have to be on the course to find them. All it takes is a curious mind, a love for the game, and a willingness to ask, "What's next?"

So as you close this book, don't think of it as the end. Think of it as just another tee shot that sets you up for countless more stories, surprises, and moments that will keep golf as unpredictable and exciting as ever.

Until next time, stay curious, stay adventurous, and remember: the best golf stories are the ones still waiting to be played.

ACKNOWLEDGEMENTS

Creating *100 Mind-Blowing Golf Facts* has been a journey of passion, patience, and a fair share of tees, greens, and driving ranges. While my name may be on the cover, this book wouldn't have come to life without the inspiration, support, and contributions from some incredible people.

First, a huge thank you to all the golf fans, storytellers, and trivia enthusiasts who've shared the wild, unpredictable, and jaw-dropping moments from the world of golf. Your love for the game and its never-ending surprises fueled every page of this book.

To my family and friends, who listened with patience (and humor) as I rambled on about hole-in-ones, impossible shots, and the strangest golf stories I could find— you're the true champions. Your support, encouragement, and laughter kept me going through every challenge.

A big thank you to my readers—you're the reason I write. Whether you're here for the laughs, the trivia, or the amazing stories of the game, this book is for you. Your curiosity and love for golf are what make these stories so special and keep golf's legacy alive.

And lastly, to the game of golf itself—thank you for being so wonderfully unpredictable. From perfect shots to wild mishaps, golf is never dull, and I'm forever grateful for the opportunity to share some of your most mind-blowing moments with the world.

Here's to golf, to the stories yet to be told, and to the game that will always keep us guessing.

ABOUT THE AUTHOR

Felix Grayson is a storyteller at heart, driven by an insatiable curiosity for the strange, surprising, and downright unpredictable moments in sports. With a passion for uncovering the wildest and most unbelievable tales from the world of golf, Felix has crafted *100 Mind-Blowing Golf Facts* to entertain, amaze, and spark wonder in fans of all ages.

When he's not diving into golf history or chasing down the next quirky golfing moment, Felix enjoys exploring courses around the world, devouring sports biographies, and pondering life's most fascinating questions over a cold drink at the 19th hole. A firm believer in the magic of the game and the power of a good story, Felix invites you to take this journey through golf's most unpredictable moments, proving that the sport is just as full of surprises off the course as it is on.

www.ingramcontent.com/pod-product-compliance
Lightning Source LLC
Chambersburg PA
CBHW030318080526
44584CB00012B/615